LIGHT

PRAYER JOURNAL

This journal belongs to:

Let There Be Light: Prayer Journal

Copyright © 2025 by Joe Benjamin
Book publishing services by Opulent Books
www.OpulentBooks.net

All rights reserved.
ISBN Paperback: 978-1-916691-70-4
ISBN Hardback: 978-1-916691-73-5
No part of this publication may be reproduced, distributed, or transmitted in any form or by any means, including photocopying, recording, or other electronic or mechanical methods, without the prior written permission of the publisher, except as permitted by copyright law. For permission requests, contact the author.

Scriptures are taken from the NEW KING JAMES VERSION® (NKJV):
Copyright© 1982 by Thomas Nelson, Inc.
Used by permission. All rights reserved.

This journal is dedicated to Light Nation. Citizens of the Light, who have embraced the call to shine brightly in a world that often tries to extinguish the flame. You are the City Lights, the ones who refuse to hide your light under a bushel.

Let there be light in all you do!

Contents

A Note from the Author v
Making the Most of This Journal vi
Week 1 1
Week 2 9
Week 3 17
Week 4 25
Week 5 33
Week 6 41
Week 7 49
Week 8 57
Week 9 65
Week 10 73
Week 11 81
Week 12 89
Week 13 97
Week 14 105
Week 15 113
Week 16 121
Week 17 129
Dreams and Visions 138
Prayer Requests and Answers 140
About the Author 144
Other related books by the author: 145

A Note from the Author

As someone who has walked through seasons of darkness and experienced the life changing power of God's Light, I understand what it means to hold on to His promises when the world feels dim. This journal is born out of a deep desire to see you step into your God-given identity as a child of the Light.

In my journey of life, I have witnessed the power of Light breaking through shadows. Whether through prayers, declarations, or sharing stories of healing and hope, I have come to understand one truth: the Light of God is unstoppable.

This journal is not merely another tool for reflection; it is a declaration. It is an invitation to let God's Light illuminate every corner of your life. It is for those who have refused to let the darkness win, for those who are determined to reflect His glory in all they do.

As you journey through these pages, I pray you will encounter the Light of His presence in fresh and powerful ways. Write boldly. Pray deeply. Reflect sincerely. And remember, your Light is meant to shine brightly for the world to see.

Your light has come!
Love and Light

Joe Benjamin

Making the Most of This Journal

Welcome to the Let There Be Light Prayer Journal! This journal is designed to help you deepen your faith, reflect on God's presence in your life, and ignite the light within you. Here's how to make the most of it:

1. **Start Each Day with Purpose**

   Begin with the Daily Pages. Write down what the Lord is saying to you, reflect on how His light is guiding you, express gratitude for His blessings, and lift up your prayers.

2. **Engage with the Weekly Check-Ins**

   At the end of each week, use the Weekly Check-In pages to reflect on your victories, challenges, and the lessons God is teaching you. Set spiritual goals to help you shine even brighter in the week ahead.

3. **Be Honest and Open**

   This journal is your personal space to connect with God. Write freely, knowing that this is a journey between you and Him.

4. **Look for God's Light Daily**

   Use the prompts and sections to intentionally seek His light in every situation, whether big or small.

5. **Use It as a Companion**

   Take this journal with you to church, Bible studies, or quiet time. Use it to capture sermon notes, scripture insights, or personal revelations.

6. **Revisit and Reflect**

   Don't just move forward, also look back. As you fill these pages, revisit them to see how God's light has been moving in your life.

This journal is your guide and friend as you walk in the light of His love and power. Let every page remind you of His faithfulness and inspire you to reflect His light to the world.

Let there be light!

Daily Pages

Date:
Write today's date in the space provided. This will help you track your journey and look back at how God has moved in your life.

Daily Scripture:
At the top of each page, you'll find a carefully selected Bible verse. Use this verse as your focus for the day. Reflect, meditate, and even memorise it to ingrain it in your heart and mind. Let it guide your prayers, thoughts, and actions throughout the day.

What Is the Lord Saying?:
Take a moment to quiet your heart and listen. Write down what you feel the Lord is speaking to you; whether through the scripture of the day, prayer, or other ways He reveals Himself. Use this section to capture God's voice in your life.

Reflection:
Use this space to record your thoughts, insights, or questions prompted by the daily scripture. Reflect on what God is teaching you, how the verse applies to your life, or anything else He places on your heart.

Today I Am Grateful For:
In this section, write down what you're thankful for today. Gratitude shifts our hearts toward God and reminds us of His goodness. List specific blessings, big or small, that you've experienced.

Prayer Points:
Write down the key things you're praying for today. This could include personal needs, intercession for others, or areas where you need God's guidance or strength.

Weekly Reflection Pages

At the end of each week, take time to pause and reflect on your journey with the weekly reflection pages. These pages are designed to help you evaluate how God has been moving in your life and prepare for the week ahead.

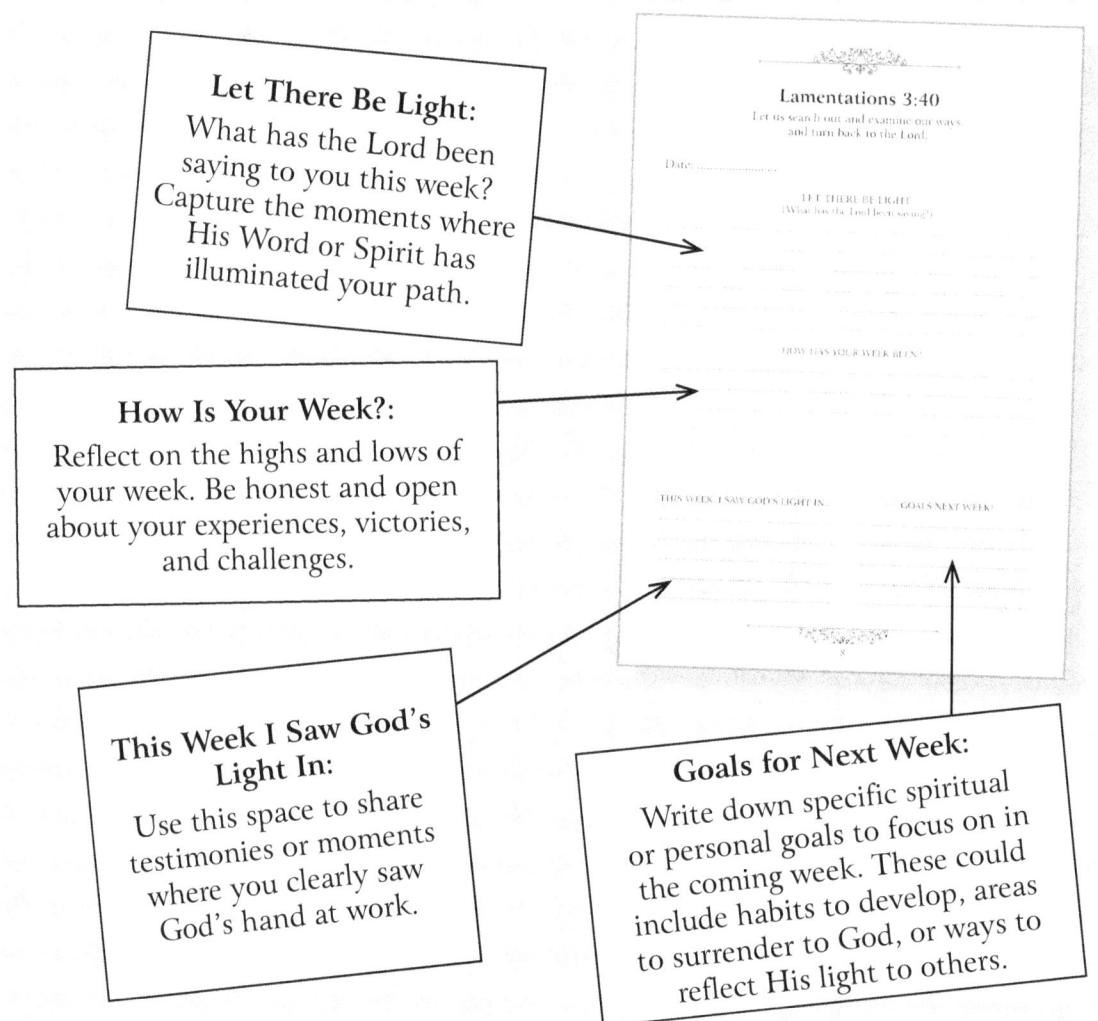

Let There Be Light:
What has the Lord been saying to you this week? Capture the moments where His Word or Spirit has illuminated your path.

How Is Your Week?:
Reflect on the highs and lows of your week. Be honest and open about your experiences, victories, and challenges.

This Week I Saw God's Light In:
Use this space to share testimonies or moments where you clearly saw God's hand at work.

Goals for Next Week:
Write down specific spiritual or personal goals to focus on in the coming week. These could include habits to develop, areas to surrender to God, or ways to reflect His light to others.

Additional Sections

1. **Prayer Requests and Answers:**

   At the back of this journal, you'll find a dedicated section to record your prayer requests. Write the date you made the request, and when God answers, record the date and how He moved. This section is a testimony of God's faithfulness and a reminder of His power.

2. **Dreams and Visions:**

   At the back of this journal, you'll find a dedicated section to record your dreams and visions. Use this space to write down any dreams you feel have spiritual significance or moments when God speaks to you through visions.

Week 1

Genesis 1:3

Then God said, "Let there be light"; and there was light.

Date: ....   Declare it: Let There Be Light!: ....

WHAT IS THE LORD SAYING?

....
....
....
....
....
....

REFLECTION

....
....
....
....
....
....

TODAY I AM GRATEFUL FOR?	PRAYER POINTS
....	....
....	....
....	....
....	....
....	....

John 8:12

Then Jesus spoke to them again, saying, "I am the light of the world. He who follows Me shall not walk in darkness, but have the light of life."

Date: ....   Declare it: Let There Be Light!: ....

WHAT IS THE LORD SAYING?

....
....
....
....
....
....

REFLECTION

....
....
....
....
....
....

TODAY I AM GRATEFUL FOR?	PRAYER POINTS
....	....
....	....
....	....
....	....
....	....

Psalm 27:1

The Lord is my light and my salvation; whom shall I fear?
The Lord is the strength of my life; of whom shall I be afraid?

Date: ....   Declare it: Let There Be Light!: ....

WHAT IS THE LORD SAYING?

....
....
....
....
....
....

REFLECTION

....
....
....
....
....
....

TODAY I AM GRATEFUL FOR?	PRAYER POINTS
....	....
....	....
....	....
....	....
....	....
....	....

Hebrews 11:1

Now faith is the substance of things hoped for,
the evidence of things not seen.

Date: ....   Declare it: Let There Be Light!: ....

WHAT IS THE LORD SAYING?

....
....
....
....
....
....

REFLECTION

....
....
....
....
....
....

TODAY I AM GRATEFUL FOR?	PRAYER POINTS
....	....
....	....
....	....
....	....
....	....
....	....

Psalm 107:1

Oh, give thanks to the Lord, for He is good!
For His mercy endures forever.

Date: ....   Declare it: Let There Be Light!: ....

WHAT IS THE LORD SAYING?

....
....
....
....
....
....

REFLECTION

....
....
....
....
....
....

TODAY I AM GRATEFUL FOR?	PRAYER POINTS
....	....
....	....
....	....
....	....
....	....
....	....

Philippians 4:6

Be anxious for nothing, but in everything by prayer and supplication, with thanksgiving, let your requests be made known to God.

Date: ....   Declare it: Let There Be Light!: ....

WHAT IS THE LORD SAYING?

....
....
....
....
....
....
....

REFLECTION

....
....
....
....
....
....
....

TODAY I AM GRATEFUL FOR?	PRAYER POINTS
....	....
....	....
....	....
....	....
....	....
....	....

Lamentations 3:40

Let us search out and examine our ways,
and turn back to the Lord.

Date: .... Declare it: Let There Be Light!: ....

WHAT HAS THE LORD BEEN SAYING?

....
....
....
....
....
....

HOW HAS YOUR WEEK BEEN?

....
....
....
....
....
....

THIS WEEK, I SAW GOD'S LIGHT IN...	GOALS NEXT WEEK!
....	....
....	....
....	....
....	....
....	....

Week 2

Matthew 5:14

You are the light of the world.
A city that is set on a hill cannot be hidden.

Date: .... Declare it: Let There Be Light!: ....

WHAT IS THE LORD SAYING?

....
....
....
....
....
....
....

REFLECTION

....
....
....
....
....
....
....

TODAY I AM GRATEFUL FOR?	PRAYER POINTS
....	....
....	....
....	....
....	....
....	....
....	....

Proverbs 3:5

Trust in the Lord with all your heart,
and lean not on your own understanding.

Date: ....   Declare it: Let There Be Light!: ....

WHAT IS THE LORD SAYING?

....
....
....
....
....
....

REFLECTION

....
....
....
....
....
....

TODAY I AM GRATEFUL FOR?	PRAYER POINTS
....	....
....	....
....	....
....	....
....	....

Psalm 100:4

Enter into His gates with thanksgiving,
and into His courts with praise.
Be thankful to Him, and bless His name.

Date: .... Declare it: Let There Be Light!: ....

WHAT IS THE LORD SAYING?

....
....
....
....
....
....

REFLECTION

....
....
....
....
....

TODAY I AM GRATEFUL FOR?   PRAYER POINTS

....
....
....
....
....
....

Jeremiah 33:3

Call to Me, and I will answer you,
and show you great and mighty things,
which you do not know.

Date: ....   Declare it: Let There Be Light!: ....

WHAT IS THE LORD SAYING?

....
....
....
....
....
....
....

REFLECTION

....
....
....
....
....
....
....

TODAY I AM GRATEFUL FOR?	PRAYER POINTS
....	....
....	....
....	....
....	....
....	....
....	....

James 1:17

Every good gift and every perfect gift is from above, and comes down from the Father of lights, with whom there is no variation or shadow of turning.

Date: .... Declare it: Let There Be Light!: ....

WHAT IS THE LORD SAYING?

....
....
....
....
....
....

REFLECTION

....
....
....
....
....
....

TODAY I AM GRATEFUL FOR?	PRAYER POINTS
....	....
....	....
....	....
....	....
....	....
....	....

2 Corinthians 5:7

For we walk by faith, not by sight.

Date: ....   Declare it: Let There Be Light!: ....

WHAT IS THE LORD SAYING?

....
....
....
....
....
....

REFLECTION

....
....
....
....
....
....

TODAY I AM GRATEFUL FOR?	PRAYER POINTS
....	....
....	....
....	....
....	....
....	....

Psalm 19:14

Let the words of my mouth and the meditation of my heart be acceptable in Your sight, O Lord, my strength and my Redeemer.

Date: ....   Declare it: Let There Be Light!: ....

WHAT HAS THE LORD BEEN SAYING?

....
....
....
....
....
....

HOW HAS YOUR WEEK BEEN?

....
....
....
....
....

THIS WEEK, I SAW GOD'S LIGHT IN...	GOALS NEXT WEEK!
....	....
....	....
....	....
....	....
....	....

Week 3

John 1:5

And the light shines in the darkness,
and the darkness did not comprehend it.

Date: .... Declare it: Let There Be Light!: ....

WHAT IS THE LORD SAYING?

....
....
....
....
....
....
....

REFLECTION

....
....
....
....
....
....

TODAY I AM GRATEFUL FOR?   PRAYER POINTS

....
....
....
....
....
....

Isaiah 41:10

Fear not, for I am with you; be not dismayed, for I am your God. I will strengthen you, yes, I will help you, I will uphold you with My righteous right hand.

Date: ....   Declare it: Let There Be Light!: ....

WHAT IS THE LORD SAYING?

....
....
....
....
....
....

REFLECTION

....
....
....
....
....
....

TODAY I AM GRATEFUL FOR?	PRAYER POINTS
....	....
....	....
....	....
....	....
....	....

1 Thessalonians 5:18

In everything give thanks; for this is the will of God in Christ Jesus for you.

Date: .... Declare it: Let There Be Light!: ....

WHAT IS THE LORD SAYING?

....
....
....
....
....
....

REFLECTION

....
....
....
....
....
....

TODAY I AM GRATEFUL FOR?	PRAYER POINTS
....	....
....	....
....	....
....	....
....	....

Matthew 7:7

Ask, and it will be given to you; seek, and you will find; knock, and it will be opened to you.

Date: ....   Declare it: Let There Be Light!: ....

WHAT IS THE LORD SAYING?

....
....
....
....
....
....

REFLECTION

....
....
....
....
....
....

TODAY I AM GRATEFUL FOR?	PRAYER POINTS
....	....
....	....
....	....
....	....
....	....

Psalm 23:1

The Lord is my shepherd; I shall not want.

Date: ....   Declare it: Let There Be Light!: ....

WHAT IS THE LORD SAYING?

....
....
....
....
....
....
....

REFLECTION

....
....
....
....
....
....
....

TODAY I AM GRATEFUL FOR?	PRAYER POINTS
....	....
....	....
....	....
....	....
....	....
....	....

Romans 10:17

So then faith comes by hearing,
and hearing by the word of God.

Date: ....   Declare it: Let There Be Light!: ....

WHAT IS THE LORD SAYING?

....
....
....
....
....
....

REFLECTION

....
....
....
....
....
....

TODAY I AM GRATEFUL FOR?	PRAYER POINTS
....	....
....	....
....	....
....	....
....	....

Psalm 139:23-24

Search me, O God, and know my heart; try me, and know my anxieties;
and see if there is any wicked way in me,
and lead me in the way everlasting.

Date: ....   Declare it: Let There Be Light!: ....

WHAT HAS THE LORD BEEN SAYING?

....
....
....
....
....
....

HOW HAS YOUR WEEK BEEN?

....
....
....
....
....
....

THIS WEEK, I SAW GOD'S LIGHT IN...	GOALS NEXT WEEK!
....	....
....	....
....	....
....	....
....	....

Week 4

Isaiah 60:1

Arise, shine; for your light has come!
And the glory of the Lord is risen upon you.

Date: ....   Declare it: Let There Be Light!: ....

WHAT IS THE LORD SAYING?

....
....
....
....
....
....
....

REFLECTION

....
....
....
....
....
....

TODAY I AM GRATEFUL FOR?	PRAYER POINTS
....	....
....	....
....	....
....	....
....	....

2 Corinthians 4:6

For it is the God who commanded light to shine out of darkness, who has shone in our hearts to give the light of the knowledge of the glory of God in the face of Jesus Christ.

Date: ....   Declare it: Let There Be Light!: ....

WHAT IS THE LORD SAYING?

....
....
....
....
....
....

REFLECTION

....
....
....
....
....
....

TODAY I AM GRATEFUL FOR?	PRAYER POINTS
....	....
....	....
....	....
....	....
....	....
....	....

Psalm 100:5

For the Lord is good; His mercy is everlasting,
and His truth endures to all generations.

Date: ....   Declare it: Let There Be Light!: ....

WHAT IS THE LORD SAYING?

....
....
....
....
....
....

REFLECTION

....
....
....
....
....
....

TODAY I AM GRATEFUL FOR?	PRAYER POINTS
....	....
....	....
....	....
....	....
....	....

James 5:16

Confess your trespasses to one another, and pray for one another, that you may be healed. The effective, fervent prayer of a righteous man avails much.

Date: ....   Declare it: Let There Be Light!: ....

WHAT IS THE LORD SAYING?

....
....
....
....
....
....

REFLECTION

....
....
....
....
....
....

TODAY I AM GRATEFUL FOR?	PRAYER POINTS
....	....
....	....
....	....
....	....
....	....
....	....

John 14:27

Peace I leave with you, My peace I give to you; not as the world gives do I give to you. Let not your heart be troubled, neither let it be afraid.

Date: ....   Declare it: Let There Be Light!: ....

WHAT IS THE LORD SAYING?

....
....
....
....
....
....

REFLECTION

....
....
....
....
....
....

TODAY I AM GRATEFUL FOR?	PRAYER POINTS
....	....
....	....
....	....
....	....
....	....

Ephesians 2:10

For we are His workmanship, created in Christ Jesus for good works, which God prepared beforehand that we should walk in them.

Date: ....   Declare it: Let There Be Light!: ....

WHAT IS THE LORD SAYING?

....
....
....
....
....
....
....

REFLECTION

....
....
....
....
....
....
....

TODAY I AM GRATEFUL FOR?	PRAYER POINTS
....	....
....	....
....	....
....	....
....	....
....	....

Proverbs 4:18

But the path of the just is like the shining sun,
that shines ever brighter unto the perfect day.

Date: ....   Declare it: Let There Be Light!: ....

WHAT HAS THE LORD BEEN SAYING?

....
....
....
....
....
....

HOW HAS YOUR WEEK BEEN?

....
....
....
....
....
....

THIS WEEK, I SAW GOD'S LIGHT IN...	GOALS NEXT WEEK!
....	....
....	....
....	....
....	....

Week 5

Matthew 5:16

Let your light so shine before men, that they may see your good works and glorify your Father in heaven.

Date: ....   Declare it: Let There Be Light!: ....

WHAT IS THE LORD SAYING?

....
....
....
....
....
....

REFLECTION

....
....
....
....
....
....

TODAY I AM GRATEFUL FOR?	PRAYER POINTS
....	....
....	....
....	....
....	....
....	....

Psalm 55:22

Cast your burden on the Lord, and He shall sustain you;
He shall never permit the righteous to be moved.

Date: ....   Declare it: Let There Be Light!: ....

WHAT IS THE LORD SAYING?

....
....
....
....
....
....

REFLECTION

....
....
....
....
....
....

TODAY I AM GRATEFUL FOR?	PRAYER POINTS
....	....
....	....
....	....
....	....
....	....
....	....

Psalm 9:1

I will praise You, O Lord, with my whole heart;
I will tell of all Your marvelous works.

Date: ....   Declare it: Let There Be Light!: ....

WHAT IS THE LORD SAYING?

....
....
....
....
....
....
....

REFLECTION

....
....
....
....
....
....

TODAY I AM GRATEFUL FOR?   PRAYER POINTS

TODAY I AM GRATEFUL FOR?	PRAYER POINTS
....	....
....	....
....	....
....	....
....	....

Colossians 4:2

Continue earnestly in prayer, being vigilant in it
with thanksgiving.

Date: ....   Declare it: Let There Be Light!: ....

WHAT IS THE LORD SAYING?

....
....
....
....
....
....
....

REFLECTION

....
....
....
....
....
....
....

TODAY I AM GRATEFUL FOR?	PRAYER POINTS
....	....
....	....
....	....
....	....
....	....
....	....

1 John 1:7

But if we walk in the light as He is in the light,
we have fellowship with one another, and the blood of
Jesus Christ His Son cleanses us from all sin.

Date: ....   Declare it: Let There Be Light!: ....

WHAT IS THE LORD SAYING?

....
....
....
....
....
....

REFLECTION

....
....
....
....
....
....

TODAY I AM GRATEFUL FOR?	PRAYER POINTS
....	....
....	....
....	....
....	....
....	....

Romans 8:28

And we know that all things work together for good to those who love God, to those who are the called according to His purpose.

Date: .... Declare it: Let There Be Light!: ....

WHAT IS THE LORD SAYING?

....
....
....
....
....
....

REFLECTION

....
....
....
....
....
....

TODAY I AM GRATEFUL FOR?	PRAYER POINTS
....	....
....	....
....	....
....	....
....	....
....	....

Lamentations 3:22-23

Through the Lord's mercies we are not consumed,
because His compassions fail not.
They are new every morning; great is Your faithfulness.

Date: ....   Declare it: Let There Be Light!: ....

WHAT HAS THE LORD BEEN SAYING?

....
....
....
....
....
....

HOW HAS YOUR WEEK BEEN?

....
....
....
....
....
....

THIS WEEK, I SAW GOD'S LIGHT IN...	GOALS NEXT WEEK!
....	....
....	....
....	....
....	....

Week 6

John 12:46

I have come as a light into the world,
that whoever believes in Me should not abide in darkness.

Date: ....   Declare it: Let There Be Light!: ....

WHAT IS THE LORD SAYING?

....
....
....
....
....
....

REFLECTION

....
....
....
....
....
....

TODAY I AM GRATEFUL FOR?	PRAYER POINTS
....	....
....	....
....	....
....	....
....	....

2 Timothy 1:7

For God has not given us a spirit of fear,
but of power and of love and of a sound mind.

Date: ....   Declare it: Let There Be Light!: ....

WHAT IS THE LORD SAYING?

....
....
....
....
....
....

REFLECTION

....
....
....
....
....
....

TODAY I AM GRATEFUL FOR?	PRAYER POINTS
....	....
....	....
....	....
....	....
....	....

Psalm 118:24

This is the day the Lord has made;
we will rejoice and be glad in it.

Date: .... Declare it: Let There Be Light!: ....

WHAT IS THE LORD SAYING?

....
....
....
....
....
....
....

REFLECTION

....
....
....
....
....
....
....

TODAY I AM GRATEFUL FOR?	PRAYER POINTS
....	....
....	....
....	....
....	....
....	....
....	....

Philippians 4:13
I can do all things through Christ who strengthens me.

Date: .... Declare it: Let There Be Light!: ....

WHAT IS THE LORD SAYING?

....
....
....
....
....
....
....

REFLECTION

....
....
....
....
....
....

TODAY I AM GRATEFUL FOR?	PRAYER POINTS
....	....
....	....
....	....
....	....
....	....
....	....

Isaiah 26:3

You will keep him in perfect peace, whose mind is stayed on You, because he trusts in You.

Date: ……………… Declare it: Let There Be Light!: ………………………………

WHAT IS THE LORD SAYING?

……………………………………………………………………………………
……………………………………………………………………………………
……………………………………………………………………………………
……………………………………………………………………………………
……………………………………………………………………………………
……………………………………………………………………………………

REFLECTION

……………………………………………………………………………………
……………………………………………………………………………………
……………………………………………………………………………………
……………………………………………………………………………………
……………………………………………………………………………………
……………………………………………………………………………………

TODAY I AM GRATEFUL FOR?	PRAYER POINTS
………………………………	………………………………
………………………………	………………………………
………………………………	………………………………
………………………………	………………………………
………………………………	………………………………

Luke 11:36

If then your whole body is full of light, having no part dark, the whole body will be full of light, as when the bright shining of a lamp gives you light.

Date: ....   Declare it: Let There Be Light!: ....

WHAT IS THE LORD SAYING?

....
....
....
....
....
....

REFLECTION

....
....
....
....
....
....

TODAY I AM GRATEFUL FOR?	PRAYER POINTS
....	....
....	....
....	....
....	....
....	....

Psalm 119:105

Your word is a lamp to my feet and a light to my path.

Date: ....   Declare it: Let There Be Light!: ....

WHAT HAS THE LORD BEEN SAYING?

....
....
....
....
....
....

HOW HAS YOUR WEEK BEEN?

....
....
....
....
....
....

THIS WEEK, I SAW GOD'S LIGHT IN...	GOALS NEXT WEEK!
....	....
....	....
....	....
....	....
....	....

Week 7

Isaiah 9:2

The people who walked in darkness have seen a great light; those who dwelt in the land of the shadow of death, upon them a light has shined.

Date: .... Declare it: Let There Be Light!: ....

WHAT IS THE LORD SAYING?

....
....
....
....
....
....

REFLECTION

....
....
....
....
....
....

TODAY I AM GRATEFUL FOR?	PRAYER POINTS
....	....
....	....
....	....
....	....
....	....

Matthew 6:33

But seek first the kingdom of God and His righteousness,
and all these things shall be added to you.

Date: ....   Declare it: Let There Be Light!: ....

WHAT IS THE LORD SAYING?

....
....
....
....
....
....

REFLECTION

....
....
....
....
....
....

TODAY I AM GRATEFUL FOR?	PRAYER POINTS
....	....
....	....
....	....
....	....
....	....
....	....

Psalm 34:1

I will bless the Lord at all times;
His praise shall continually be in my mouth.

Date: .... Declare it: Let There Be Light!: ....

WHAT IS THE LORD SAYING?

....
....
....
....
....
....

REFLECTION

....
....
....
....
....
....

TODAY I AM GRATEFUL FOR?	PRAYER POINTS
....	....
....	....
....	....
....	....
....	....
....	....

Mark 11:24

Therefore I say to you, whatever things you ask when you pray, believe that you receive them, and you will have them.

Date: ....   Declare it: Let There Be Light!: ....

WHAT IS THE LORD SAYING?

....
....
....
....
....
....

REFLECTION

....
....
....
....
....
....

TODAY I AM GRATEFUL FOR?	PRAYER POINTS
....	....
....	....
....	....
....	....
....	....
....	....

Hebrews 13:8
Jesus Christ is the same yesterday, today, and forever.

Date: .... Declare it: Let There Be Light!: ....

WHAT IS THE LORD SAYING?

....
....
....
....
....
....
....

REFLECTION

....
....
....
....
....
....

TODAY I AM GRATEFUL FOR?	PRAYER POINTS
....	....
....	....
....	....
....	....
....	....
....	....

Ephesians 3:20

Now to Him who is able to do exceedingly abundantly above all that we ask or think, according to the power that works in us.

Date: ....   Declare it: Let There Be Light!: ....

WHAT IS THE LORD SAYING?

....
....
....
....
....
....

REFLECTION

....
....
....
....
....
....

TODAY I AM GRATEFUL FOR?	PRAYER POINTS
....	....
....	....
....	....
....	....
....	....

Psalm 90:12

So teach us to number our days,
that we may gain a heart of wisdom.

Date: ....   Declare it: Let There Be Light!: ....

WHAT HAS THE LORD BEEN SAYING?

....
....
....
....
....
....

HOW HAS YOUR WEEK BEEN?

....
....
....
....
....
....

THIS WEEK, I SAW GOD'S LIGHT IN...	GOALS NEXT WEEK!
....	....
....	....
....	....
....	....
....	....

Week 8

John 3:19

And this is the condemnation, that the light has come into the world, and men loved darkness rather than light, because their deeds were evil.

Date: .... Declare it: Let There Be Light!: ....

WHAT IS THE LORD SAYING?

....
....
....
....
....
....

REFLECTION

....
....
....
....
....
....

TODAY I AM GRATEFUL FOR?	PRAYER POINTS
....	....
....	....
....	....
....	....
....	....

1 Corinthians 16:13
Watch, stand fast in the faith, be brave, be strong.

Date: .... Declare it: Let There Be Light!: ....

WHAT IS THE LORD SAYING?

....
....
....
....
....
....

REFLECTION

....
....
....
....
....
....

TODAY I AM GRATEFUL FOR?   PRAYER POINTS

....
....
....
....
....

Psalm 145:1

I will extol You, my God, O King; and I will bless Your name forever and ever.

Date: ....   Declare it: Let There Be Light!: ....

WHAT IS THE LORD SAYING?

....
....
....
....
....
....

REFLECTION

....
....
....
....
....
....

TODAY I AM GRATEFUL FOR?	PRAYER POINTS
....	....
....	....
....	....
....	....
....	....

Matthew 18:19-20

Again I say to you that if two of you agree on earth concerning anything that they ask, it will be done for them by My Father in heaven. For where two or three are gathered together in My name, I am there in the midst of them.

Date: .... Declare it: Let There Be Light!: ....

WHAT IS THE LORD SAYING?

....
....
....
....
....
....
....

REFLECTION

....
....
....
....
....
....
....

TODAY I AM GRATEFUL FOR?	PRAYER POINTS
....	....
....	....
....	....
....	....
....	....

Proverbs 16:9

A man's heart plans his way, but the Lord directs his steps.

Date: ....   Declare it: Let There Be Light!: ....

WHAT IS THE LORD SAYING?

....
....
....
....
....
....

REFLECTION

....
....
....
....
....
....

TODAY I AM GRATEFUL FOR?	PRAYER POINTS
....	....
....	....
....	....
....	....
....	....
....	....

2 Corinthians 12:9

And He said to me, "My grace is sufficient for you, for My strength is made perfect in weakness."

Date: ....   Declare it: Let There Be Light!: ....

WHAT IS THE LORD SAYING?

....
....
....
....
....
....
....

REFLECTION

....
....
....
....
....
....
....

TODAY I AM GRATEFUL FOR?	PRAYER POINTS
....	....
....	....
....	....
....	....
....	....

James 1:22

But be doers of the word, and not hearers only, deceiving yourselves.

Date: ....   Declare it: Let There Be Light!: ....

WHAT HAS THE LORD BEEN SAYING?

....
....
....
....
....
....

HOW HAS YOUR WEEK BEEN?

....
....
....
....
....
....

THIS WEEK, I SAW GOD'S LIGHT IN...	GOALS NEXT WEEK!
....	....
....	....
....	....
....	....
....	....

Week 9

John 11:9

Jesus answered, "Are there not twelve hours in the day? If anyone walks in the day, he does not stumble, because he sees the light of this world."

Date: ....   Declare it: Let There Be Light!: ....

WHAT IS THE LORD SAYING?

....
....
....
....
....
....

REFLECTION

....
....
....
....
....
....

TODAY I AM GRATEFUL FOR?	PRAYER POINTS
....	....
....	....
....	....
....	....
....	....
....	....

Isaiah 40:31

But those who wait on the Lord shall renew their strength; they shall mount up with wings like eagles, they shall run and not be weary, they shall walk and not faint.

Date: ....　　Declare it: Let There Be Light!: ....

WHAT IS THE LORD SAYING?

....
....
....
....
....
....

REFLECTION

....
....
....
....
....
....

TODAY I AM GRATEFUL FOR?	PRAYER POINTS
....	....
....	....
....	....
....	....
....	....
....	....

Psalm 95:2

Let us come before His presence with thanksgiving;
let us shout joyfully to Him with psalms.

Date: ....   Declare it: Let There Be Light!: ....

WHAT IS THE LORD SAYING?

....
....
....
....
....
....

REFLECTION

....
....
....
....
....
....

TODAY I AM GRATEFUL FOR?	PRAYER POINTS
....	....
....	....
....	....
....	....
....	....

1 Peter 5:7

Casting all your care upon Him, for He cares for you.

Date: ....   Declare it: Let There Be Light!: ....

WHAT IS THE LORD SAYING?

....
....
....
....
....
....
....

REFLECTION

....
....
....
....
....
....
....

TODAY I AM GRATEFUL FOR?	PRAYER POINTS
....	....
....	....
....	....
....	....
....	....

Philippians 1:6

Being confident of this very thing, that He who has begun a good work in you will complete it until the day of Jesus Christ.

Date: .... Declare it: Let There Be Light!: ....

WHAT IS THE LORD SAYING?

....
....
....
....
....
....
....

REFLECTION

....
....
....
....
....
....
....

TODAY I AM GRATEFUL FOR?	PRAYER POINTS
....	....
....	....
....	....
....	....
....	....

Colossians 3:17

And whatever you do in word or deed, do all in the name of the Lord Jesus, giving thanks to God the Father through Him.

Date: .... Declare it: Let There Be Light!: ....

WHAT IS THE LORD SAYING?

....
....
....
....
....
....

REFLECTION

....
....
....
....
....
....

TODAY I AM GRATEFUL FOR?	PRAYER POINTS
....	....
....	....
....	....
....	....
....	....

Psalm 119:18

Open my eyes, that I may see wondrous things from Your law.

Date: .... Declare it: Let There Be Light!: ....

WHAT HAS THE LORD BEEN SAYING?

....
....
....
....
....
....

HOW HAS YOUR WEEK BEEN?

....
....
....
....
....
....

THIS WEEK, I SAW GOD'S LIGHT IN…	GOALS NEXT WEEK!
....	....
....	....
....	....
....	....
....	....

Week 10

Ephesians 5:8

For you were once darkness, but now you are light in the Lord. Walk as children of light.

Date: .... Declare it: Let There Be Light!: ....

WHAT IS THE LORD SAYING?

....
....
....
....
....
....

REFLECTION

....
....
....
....
....
....

TODAY I AM GRATEFUL FOR?	PRAYER POINTS
....	....
....	....
....	....
....	....
....	....

Romans 15:13

Now may the God of hope fill you with all joy and peace in believing, that you may abound in hope by the power of the Holy Spirit.

Date: ....   Declare it: Let There Be Light!: ....

WHAT IS THE LORD SAYING?

....
....
....
....
....
....

REFLECTION

....
....
....
....
....
....

TODAY I AM GRATEFUL FOR?	PRAYER POINTS
....	....
....	....
....	....
....	....
....	....
....	....

Psalm 30:4

Sing praise to the Lord, you saints of His, and give thanks at the remembrance of His holy name.

Date: .... Declare it: Let There Be Light!: ....

WHAT IS THE LORD SAYING?

....
....
....
....
....
....

REFLECTION

....
....
....
....
....
....

TODAY I AM GRATEFUL FOR?	PRAYER POINTS
....	....
....	....
....	....
....	....
....	....
....	....

Matthew 26:41

Watch and pray, lest you enter into temptation.
The spirit indeed is willing, but the flesh is weak.

Date: .... Declare it: Let There Be Light!: ....

WHAT IS THE LORD SAYING?

....
....
....
....
....
....
....

REFLECTION

....
....
....
....
....
....

TODAY I AM GRATEFUL FOR?	PRAYER POINTS
....	....
....	....
....	....
....	....
....	....
....	....

John 15:5

I am the vine, you are the branches. He who abides in Me, and I in him, bears much fruit; for without Me you can do nothing.

Date: ....   Declare it: Let There Be Light!: ....

WHAT IS THE LORD SAYING?

....
....
....
....
....
....

REFLECTION

....
....
....
....
....
....

TODAY I AM GRATEFUL FOR?	PRAYER POINTS
....	....
....	....
....	....
....	....
....	....

Isaiah 43:2

When you pass through the waters, I will be with you; and through the rivers, they shall not overflow you. When you walk through the fire, you shall not be burned, nor shall the flame scorch you.

Date: ....   Declare it: Let There Be Light!: ....

WHAT IS THE LORD SAYING?

....
....
....
....
....
....

REFLECTION

....
....
....
....
....
....

TODAY I AM GRATEFUL FOR?	PRAYER POINTS
....	....
....	....
....	....
....	....
....	....

Proverbs 3:6

In all your ways acknowledge Him, and He shall direct your paths.

Date: ....   Declare it: Let There Be Light!: ....

WHAT HAS THE LORD BEEN SAYING?

....
....
....
....
....
....

HOW HAS YOUR WEEK BEEN?

....
....
....
....
....
....

THIS WEEK, I SAW GOD'S LIGHT IN...	GOALS NEXT WEEK!
....	....
....	....
....	....
....	....

Week 11

2 Samuel 22:29

For You are my lamp, O Lord; the Lord shall enlighten my darkness.

Date: ....   Declare it: Let There Be Light!: ....

WHAT IS THE LORD SAYING?

....
....
....
....
....
....
....

REFLECTION

....
....
....
....
....
....

TODAY I AM GRATEFUL FOR?	PRAYER POINTS
....	....
....	....
....	....
....	....
....	....

Hebrews 12:2

Looking unto Jesus, the author and finisher of our faith, who for the joy that was set before Him endured the cross, despising the shame, and has sat down at the right hand of the throne of God.

Date: ....   Declare it: Let There Be Light!: ....

WHAT IS THE LORD SAYING?

....
....
....
....
....
....

REFLECTION

....
....
....
....
....
....

TODAY I AM GRATEFUL FOR?	PRAYER POINTS
....	....
....	....
....	....
....	....
....	....

Psalm 136:1

Oh, give thanks to the Lord, for He is good!
For His mercy endures forever.

Date: ....   Declare it: Let There Be Light!: ....

WHAT IS THE LORD SAYING?

....
....
....
....
....
....

REFLECTION

....
....
....
....
....
....

TODAY I AM GRATEFUL FOR?	PRAYER POINTS
....	....
....	....
....	....
....	....
....	....

Luke 18:1

Then He spoke a parable to them, that men always ought to pray and not lose heart.

Date: ....   Declare it: Let There Be Light!: ....

WHAT IS THE LORD SAYING?

....
....
....
....
....
....
....

REFLECTION

....
....
....
....
....
....

TODAY I AM GRATEFUL FOR?	PRAYER POINTS
....	....
....	....
....	....
....	....
....	....
....	....

Psalm 46:10

Be still, and know that I am God; I will be exalted among the nations, I will be exalted in the earth!

Date: ....   Declare it: Let There Be Light!: ....

WHAT IS THE LORD SAYING?

....
....
....
....
....
....

REFLECTION

....
....
....
....
....
....

TODAY I AM GRATEFUL FOR?	PRAYER POINTS
....	....
....	....
....	....
....	....
....	....

Romans 8:38-39

For I am persuaded that neither death nor life, nor angels nor principalities nor powers, nor things present nor things to come, nor height nor depth, nor any other created thing, shall be able to separate us from the love of God which is in Christ Jesus our Lord.

Date: ....   Declare it: Let There Be Light!: ....

WHAT IS THE LORD SAYING?

....
....
....
....
....
....

REFLECTION

....
....
....
....
....
....

TODAY I AM GRATEFUL FOR?	PRAYER POINTS
....	....
....	....
....	....
....	....
....	....

Micah 6:8

He has shown you, O man, what is good; and what does the Lord require of you but to do justly, to love mercy, and to walk humbly with your God?

Date: ....   Declare it: Let There Be Light!: ....

WHAT HAS THE LORD BEEN SAYING?

....
....
....
....
....
....

HOW HAS YOUR WEEK BEEN?

....
....
....
....
....
....

THIS WEEK, I SAW GOD'S LIGHT IN...	GOALS NEXT WEEK!
....	....
....	....
....	....
....	....
....	....

Week 12

Psalm 37:6

He shall bring forth your righteousness as the light,
and your justice as the noonday.

Date: ....   Declare it: Let There Be Light!: ....

WHAT IS THE LORD SAYING?

....
....
....
....
....
....
....

REFLECTION

....
....
....
....
....
....
....

TODAY I AM GRATEFUL FOR?	PRAYER POINTS
....	....
....	....
....	....
....	....
....	....
....	....

1 Corinthians 10:13

No temptation has overtaken you except such as is common to man; but God is faithful, who will not allow you to be tempted beyond what you are able, but with the temptation will also make the way of escape, that you may be able to bear it.

Date: .... Declare it: Let There Be Light!: ....

WHAT IS THE LORD SAYING?

....
....
....
....
....
....

REFLECTION

....
....
....
....
....
....

TODAY I AM GRATEFUL FOR?	PRAYER POINTS
....	....
....	....
....	....
....	....
....	....
....	....

Psalm 92:1

It is good to give thanks to the Lord, and to sing praises to Your name, O Most High.

Date: ....   Declare it: Let There Be Light!: ....

WHAT IS THE LORD SAYING?

....
....
....
....
....
....

REFLECTION

....
....
....
....
....
....

TODAY I AM GRATEFUL FOR?	PRAYER POINTS
....	....
....	....
....	....
....	....
....	....
....	....

Mark 1:35

Now in the morning, having risen a long while before daylight, He went out and departed to a solitary place; and there He prayed.

Date: .... Declare it: Let There Be Light!: ....

WHAT IS THE LORD SAYING?

....
....
....
....
....
....

REFLECTION

....
....
....
....
....
....

TODAY I AM GRATEFUL FOR?	PRAYER POINTS
....	....
....	....
....	....
....	....
....	....
....	....

John 10:10

The thief does not come except to steal, and to kill, and to destroy. I have come that they may have life, and that they may have it more abundantly.

Date: ....   Declare it: Let There Be Light!: ....

WHAT IS THE LORD SAYING?

....
....
....
....
....
....

REFLECTION

....
....
....
....
....
....

TODAY I AM GRATEFUL FOR?	PRAYER POINTS
....	....
....	....
....	....
....	....
....	....

Psalm 121:1-2

I will lift up my eyes to the hills – from whence comes my help?
My help comes from the Lord, who made heaven and earth.

Date: ....   Declare it: Let There Be Light!: ....

WHAT IS THE LORD SAYING?

....
....
....
....
....
....

REFLECTION

....
....
....
....
....
....

TODAY I AM GRATEFUL FOR?	PRAYER POINTS
....	....
....	....
....	....
....	....
....	....

Galatians 6:9

And let us not grow weary while doing good, for in due season we shall reap if we do not lose heart.

Date: .... Declare it: Let There Be Light!: ....

WHAT HAS THE LORD BEEN SAYING?

....
....
....
....
....
....

HOW HAS YOUR WEEK BEEN?

....
....
....
....
....
....

THIS WEEK, I SAW GOD'S LIGHT IN...	GOALS NEXT WEEK!
....	....
....	....
....	....
....	....
....	....

Week 13

Matthew 4:16

The people who sat in darkness have seen a great light, and upon those who sat in the region and shadow of death light has dawned.

Date: .... Declare it: Let There Be Light!: ....

WHAT IS THE LORD SAYING?

....
....
....
....
....
....
....

REFLECTION

....
....
....
....
....
....
....

TODAY I AM GRATEFUL FOR?	PRAYER POINTS
....	....
....	....
....	....
....	....
....	....

Joshua 1:9

Have I not commanded you? Be strong and of good courage;
do not be afraid, nor be dismayed, for the Lord your God is with you
wherever you go.

Date: ....   Declare it: Let There Be Light!: ....

WHAT IS THE LORD SAYING?

....
....
....
....
....
....

REFLECTION

....
....
....
....
....
....

TODAY I AM GRATEFUL FOR?	PRAYER POINTS
....	....
....	....
....	....
....	....
....	....
....	....

1 Chronicles 16:34

Oh, give thanks to the Lord, for He is good!
For His mercy endures forever.

Date: .... Declare it: Let There Be Light!: ....

WHAT IS THE LORD SAYING?

....
....
....
....
....
....

REFLECTION

....
....
....
....
....
....

TODAY I AM GRATEFUL FOR?	PRAYER POINTS
....	....
....	....
....	....
....	....
....	....

Psalm 34:15

The eyes of the Lord are on the righteous,
and His ears are open to their cry.

Date: ....   Declare it: Let There Be Light!: ....

WHAT IS THE LORD SAYING?

....
....
....
....
....
....

REFLECTION

....
....
....
....
....
....

TODAY I AM GRATEFUL FOR?	PRAYER POINTS
....	....
....	....
....	....
....	....
....	....
....	....

Isaiah 55:6

Seek the Lord while He may be found,
call upon Him while He is near.

Date: .... Declare it: Let There Be Light!: ....

WHAT IS THE LORD SAYING?

....
....
....
....
....
....

REFLECTION

....
....
....
....
....

TODAY I AM GRATEFUL FOR?	PRAYER POINTS
....	....
....	....
....	....
....	....
....	....
....	....

Romans 12:12

Rejoicing in hope, patient in tribulation,
continuing steadfastly in prayer.

Date: ....   Declare it: Let There Be Light!: ....

WHAT IS THE LORD SAYING?

....
....
....
....
....
....

REFLECTION

....
....
....
....
....
....

TODAY I AM GRATEFUL FOR?	PRAYER POINTS
....	....
....	....
....	....
....	....
....	....

Psalm 16:11

You will show me the path of life; in Your presence is fullness of joy; at Your right hand are pleasures forevermore.

Date: ....   Declare it: Let There Be Light!: ....

WHAT HAS THE LORD BEEN SAYING?

....
....
....
....
....
....

HOW HAS YOUR WEEK BEEN?

....
....
....
....
....
....

THIS WEEK, I SAW GOD'S LIGHT IN...	GOALS NEXT WEEK!
....	....
....	....
....	....
....	....
....	....

Week 14

Ephesians 5:14

Therefore He says: "Awake, you who sleep, arise from the dead, and Christ will give you light."

Date: ....   Declare it: Let There Be Light!: ....

WHAT IS THE LORD SAYING?

....
....
....
....
....
....

REFLECTION

....
....
....
....
....
....

TODAY I AM GRATEFUL FOR?	PRAYER POINTS
....	....
....	....
....	....
....	....
....	....

Isaiah 26:4

Trust in the Lord forever, for in Yah, the Lord,
is everlasting strength.

Date: .... Declare it: Let There Be Light!: ....

WHAT IS THE LORD SAYING?

....
....
....
....
....
....

REFLECTION

....
....
....
....
....
....

TODAY I AM GRATEFUL FOR?	PRAYER POINTS
....	....
....	....
....	....
....	....
....	....

Colossians 3:15

And let the peace of God rule in your hearts, to which also you were called in one body; and be thankful.

Date: .... Declare it: Let There Be Light!: ....

WHAT IS THE LORD SAYING?

....
....
....
....
....
....

REFLECTION

....
....
....
....
....
....

TODAY I AM GRATEFUL FOR?	PRAYER POINTS
....	....
....	....
....	....
....	....
....	....

Luke 6:12

Now it came to pass in those days that He went out to the mountain to pray, and continued all night in prayer to God.

Date: ....   Declare it: Let There Be Light!: ....

WHAT IS THE LORD SAYING?

....
....
....
....
....
....
....

REFLECTION

....
....
....
....
....
....
....

TODAY I AM GRATEFUL FOR?	PRAYER POINTS
....	....
....	....
....	....
....	....
....	....
....	....

2 Timothy 4:7

I have fought the good fight, I have finished the race,
I have kept the faith.

Date: ....   Declare it: Let There Be Light!: ....

WHAT IS THE LORD SAYING?

....
....
....
....
....
....

REFLECTION

....
....
....
....
....
....

TODAY I AM GRATEFUL FOR?	PRAYER POINTS
....	....
....	....
....	....
....	....
....	....

Psalm 145:9

The Lord is good to all, and His tender mercies are over all His works.

Date: .... Declare it: Let There Be Light!: ....

WHAT IS THE LORD SAYING?

....
....
....
....
....
....

REFLECTION

....
....
....
....
....
....

TODAY I AM GRATEFUL FOR?	PRAYER POINTS
....	....
....	....
....	....
....	....
....	....

Proverbs 16:3

Commit your works to the Lord,
and your thoughts will be established.

Date: ....   Declare it: Let There Be Light!: ....

WHAT HAS THE LORD BEEN SAYING?

....
....
....
....
....
....

HOW HAS YOUR WEEK BEEN?

....
....
....
....
....
....

THIS WEEK, I SAW GOD'S LIGHT IN...	GOALS NEXT WEEK!
....	....
....	....
....	....
....	....
....	....

Week 15

John 12:35

Then Jesus said to them, "A little while longer the light is with you. Walk while you have the light, lest darkness overtake you; he who walks in darkness does not know where he is going."

Date: ....   Declare it: Let There Be Light!: ....

WHAT IS THE LORD SAYING?

....
....
....
....
....
....

REFLECTION

....
....
....
....
....
....

TODAY I AM GRATEFUL FOR?	PRAYER POINTS
....	....
....	....
....	....
....	....
....	....
....	....

Hebrews 10:23

Let us hold fast the confession of our hope without wavering,
for He who promised is faithful.

Date: ....   Declare it: Let There Be Light!: ....

WHAT IS THE LORD SAYING?

....
....
....
....
....
....

REFLECTION

....
....
....
....
....
....

TODAY I AM GRATEFUL FOR?	PRAYER POINTS
....	....
....	....
....	....
....	....
....	....
....	....

Psalm 28:7

The Lord is my strength and my shield; my heart trusted in Him, and I am helped; therefore my heart greatly rejoices, and with my song I will praise Him.

Date: .... Declare it: Let There Be Light!: ....

WHAT IS THE LORD SAYING?

....
....
....
....
....
....

REFLECTION

....
....
....
....
....
....

TODAY I AM GRATEFUL FOR?	PRAYER POINTS
....	....
....	....
....	....
....	....
....	....
....	....

Matthew 21:22

And whatever things you ask in prayer,
believing, you will receive.

Date: ....   Declare it: Let There Be Light!: ....

WHAT IS THE LORD SAYING?

....
....
....
....
....
....
....

REFLECTION

....
....
....
....
....
....
....

TODAY I AM GRATEFUL FOR?	PRAYER POINTS
....	....
....	....
....	....
....	....
....	....
....	....

Psalm 119:11

Your word I have hidden in my heart,
that I might not sin against You.

Date: .... Declare it: Let There Be Light!: ....

WHAT IS THE LORD SAYING?

....
....
....
....
....
....
....

REFLECTION

....
....
....
....
....
....

TODAY I AM GRATEFUL FOR?	PRAYER POINTS
....	....
....	....
....	....
....	....
....	....
....	....

1 Peter 2:9

But you are a chosen generation, a royal priesthood, a holy nation, His own special people, that you may proclaim the praises of Him who called you out of darkness into His marvelous light.

Date: ....   Declare it: Let There Be Light!: ....

WHAT IS THE LORD SAYING?

....
....
....
....
....
....

REFLECTION

....
....
....
....
....
....

TODAY I AM GRATEFUL FOR?	PRAYER POINTS
....	....
....	....
....	....
....	....
....	....
....	....

Psalm 37:5

Commit your way to the Lord, trust also in Him,
and He shall bring it to pass.

Date: ....   Declare it: Let There Be Light!: ....

WHAT HAS THE LORD BEEN SAYING?

....
....
....
....
....
....

HOW HAS YOUR WEEK BEEN?

....
....
....
....
....
....

THIS WEEK, I SAW GOD'S LIGHT IN...	GOALS NEXT WEEK!
....	....
....	....
....	....
....	....

Week 16

Isaiah 58:8

Then your light shall break forth like the morning, your healing shall spring forth speedily, and your righteousness shall go before you; the glory of the Lord shall be your rear guard.

Date: ....   Declare it: Let There Be Light!: ....

WHAT IS THE LORD SAYING?

....
....
....
....
....
....

REFLECTION

....
....
....
....
....
....

TODAY I AM GRATEFUL FOR?	PRAYER POINTS
....	....
....	....
....	....
....	....
....	....

Mark 9:23

Jesus said to him, "If you can believe,
all things are possible to him who believes."

Date: ....   Declare it: Let There Be Light!: ....

WHAT IS THE LORD SAYING?

....
....
....
....
....
....
....

REFLECTION

....
....
....
....
....
....

TODAY I AM GRATEFUL FOR?	PRAYER POINTS
....	....
....	....
....	....
....	....
....	....
....	....

Psalm 136:26

Oh, give thanks to the God of heaven!
For His mercy endures forever.

Date: .... Declare it: Let There Be Light!: ....

WHAT IS THE LORD SAYING?

....
....
....
....
....
....

REFLECTION

....
....
....
....
....
....

TODAY I AM GRATEFUL FOR?	PRAYER POINTS
....	....
....	....
....	....
....	....
....	....

James 4:8

Draw near to God and He will draw near to you. Cleanse your hands, you sinners; and purify your hearts, you double-minded.

Date: ....   Declare it: Let There Be Light!: ....

WHAT IS THE LORD SAYING?

....
....
....
....
....
....

REFLECTION

....
....
....
....
....
....

TODAY I AM GRATEFUL FOR?	PRAYER POINTS
....	....
....	....
....	....
....	....
....	....
....	....

Proverbs 16:20

He who heeds the word wisely will find good,
and whoever trusts in the Lord, happy is he.

Date: ....   Declare it: Let There Be Light!: ....

WHAT IS THE LORD SAYING?

....
....
....
....
....
....

REFLECTION

....
....
....
....
....
....

TODAY I AM GRATEFUL FOR?	PRAYER POINTS
....	....
....	....
....	....
....	....
....	....

Psalm 62:8

Trust in Him at all times, you people; pour out your heart before Him; God is a refuge for us.

Date: ....   Declare it: Let There Be Light!: ....

WHAT IS THE LORD SAYING?

....
....
....
....
....
....
....

REFLECTION

....
....
....
....
....
....

TODAY I AM GRATEFUL FOR?	PRAYER POINTS
....	....
....	....
....	....
....	....
....	....

Matthew 6:9-10

In this manner, therefore, pray: Our Father in heaven, hallowed be Your name. Your kingdom come. Your will be done on earth as it is in heaven.

Date: ....   Declare it: Let There Be Light!: ....

WHAT HAS THE LORD BEEN SAYING?

....
....
....
....
....
....

HOW HAS YOUR WEEK BEEN?

....
....
....
....
....
....

THIS WEEK, I SAW GOD'S LIGHT IN...	GOALS NEXT WEEK!
....	....
....	....
....	....
....	....
....	....

Week 17

Revelation 22:5

There shall be no night there: They need no lamp nor light of the sun, for the Lord God gives them light. And they shall reign forever and ever.

Date: .... Declare it: Let There Be Light!: ....

WHAT IS THE LORD SAYING?

....
....
....
....
....
....
....

REFLECTION

....
....
....
....
....
....

TODAY I AM GRATEFUL FOR?	PRAYER POINTS
....	....
....	....
....	....
....	....
....	....

2 Corinthians 5:17

Therefore, if anyone is in Christ, he is a new creation; old things have passed away; behold, all things have become new.

Date: ....   Declare it: Let There Be Light!: ....

WHAT IS THE LORD SAYING?

....
....
....
....
....
....

REFLECTION

....
....
....
....
....
....

TODAY I AM GRATEFUL FOR?	PRAYER POINTS
....	....
....	....
....	....
....	....
....	....

Psalm 118:1

Oh, give thanks to the Lord, for He is good!
For His mercy endures forever.

Date: .... Declare it: Let There Be Light!: ....

WHAT IS THE LORD SAYING?

....
....
....
....
....
....

REFLECTION

....
....
....
....
....
....

TODAY I AM GRATEFUL FOR?	PRAYER POINTS
....	....
....	....
....	....
....	....
....	....

1 Thessalonians 5:17
Pray without ceasing.

Date: ....   Declare it: Let There Be Light!: ....

WHAT IS THE LORD SAYING?

....
....
....
....
....
....

REFLECTION

....
....
....
....
....
....

TODAY I AM GRATEFUL FOR?	PRAYER POINTS
....	....
....	....
....	....
....	....
....	....

Isaiah 40:8

The grass withers, the flower fades,
but the word of our God stands forever.

Date: ....   Declare it: Let There Be Light!: ....

WHAT IS THE LORD SAYING?

....
....
....
....
....
....
....

REFLECTION

....
....
....
....
....
....
....

TODAY I AM GRATEFUL FOR?	PRAYER POINTS
....	....
....	....
....	....
....	....
....	....

Romans 8:31

What then shall we say to these things?
If God is for us, who can be against us?

Date: ....   Declare it: Let There Be Light!: ....

WHAT IS THE LORD SAYING?

....
....
....
....
....
....

REFLECTION

....
....
....
....
....
....

TODAY I AM GRATEFUL FOR?	PRAYER POINTS
....	....
....	....
....	....
....	....
....	....
....	....

Psalm 150:6

Let everything that has breath praise the Lord. Praise the Lord!

Date: .... Declare it: Let There Be Light!: ....

WHAT HAS THE LORD BEEN SAYING?

....
....
....
....
....
....

HOW HAS YOUR WEEK BEEN?

....
....
....
....
....
....

THIS WEEK, I SAW GOD'S LIGHT IN...	GOALS NEXT WEEK!
....	....
....	....
....	....
....	....

Revelation 21:23

The city had no need of the sun or of the moon to shine in it, for the glory of God illuminated it. The Lamb is its light.

Date: ....   Declare it: Let There Be Light!: ....

WHAT IS THE LORD SAYING?

....
....
....
....
....
....

REFLECTION

....
....
....
....
....
....

TODAY I AM GRATEFUL FOR?	PRAYER POINTS
....	....
....	....
....	....
....	....
....	....
....	....

Dreams and Visions

Dreams and Visions

Prayer Requests and Answers

Prayer Request	Prayer Date	Date Answered
....	....	....
....	....	....
....	....	....
....	....	....
....	....	....
....	....	....
....	....	....
....	....	....
....	....	....
....	....	....
....	....	....
....	....	....
....	....	....
....	....	....
....	....	....
....	....	....
....	....	....
....	....	....
....	....	....
....	....	....
....	....	....
....	....	....
....	....	....
....	....	....
....	....	....
....	....	....
....	....	....
....	....	....

Prayer Requests and Answers

Prayer Request	Prayer Date	Date Answered

Notes

About the Author

 Joe Benjamin is a speaker, author, songwriter, entrepreneur, and seasoned business strategist and coach, dedicated to empowering believers for impactful leadership in the marketplace. He believes that the marketplace is the new battleground for spiritual warfare, where God is positioning His people as influential leaders to shape culture and bring transformation.

As the founder of Light Nation, Joe has created a global dynamic platform designed to equip end-time believers to recognise their unique purpose and confidently walk in their divine light.

Joe is married to his beloved wife, Josie, and together they are blessed with two children, Jael Jovanna and Joseph Benjamin III. The couple is renowned for their visionary leadership, innovation, and boldness. Joe and Josie are highly sought-after international conference speakers, inspiring audiences worldwide with their compelling messages and insights.

Visit Joe Benjamin's website here: www.JoeBenjamin.org

Other related books by the author:

This book gives you some practical insights on how you can live a LIFESTYLE OF PRAYER.
This revelation was born out of the womb of much prayer and fasting. The writer deals with important questions about prayer head-on. What does it mean to pray without ceasing? What are the ingredients of revival?

Available on Amazon

www.ingramcontent.com/pod-product-compliance
Lightning Source LLC
Chambersburg PA
CBHW081710100526
44590CB00022B/3717